A HISTORY OF
THE KENT FAMILY
of Potsdam, New York

A HISTORY OF
THE KENT FAMILY
of Potsdam, New York

PATRICIA R. MIHOK

ISBN 978-0-9915738-5-1

I would like to thank my cousin, Bruce Kent, for providing me with photographs and other information regarding the Kent family and his support for this project.

Contents

Preface

This history is an exploration of my mother's side of my family. Alberta Jane Kent was the only daughter of Albert Byron Kent and Catherine Newcomb Gardner. Jane often talked about writing about her family history, but never actually did. Apparently, I have taken over where she left off.

My journey into the family history began seven years ago and has been an on and off project. I can certainly understand how my mother never completed the job as she did not have a computer with access to the internet. I would have never been able to have done the research needed without that access.

It has been enlightening to see how the Kent family has been part of the history of the United States since the first settlers arrived here from England in the 1600s. They came from the English middle class that was really the backbone of Old England to prosper in a land where they could be free from political, economic and religious constraints. They participated in every aspect, good and bad, that has made the United States the country that it is today.

The information I present is as accurate as possible based on the material available at this time. As more documents are found, I expect that updates will be necessary.

The Kents of Old England

John Kent, date and place of birth unknown, made his will on 15 March 1527. In it he mentions his wife Johan and a son Thomas. At the time of his death he was residing in Nether Wallop, Hampshire, England.

John's will does not list his occupation or items that could be used to suggest an occupation. He does bequeath sums of money and asks that his wife recover debts owed him. The sums do not appear large.

As John requested to be buried in the churchyard of St. Andrews in Lower (Nether) Wallop, he can be assumed to be Catholic. Henry VIII did not officially break with the Catholic Church to create the Church of England until 1534.

John Kent and wife Johan had at least two children, Nicholas and Thomas.

Thomas Kent was born about 1500 probably in Nether Wallop, Hampshire, England, but there is no direct evidence for that. He made his will on 31 October 1558 and the inventory of his estate was done on 28 November 1558. Apparently his brother Nicholas died about six months before him. Thomas's will mentions his wife, Christian, date and place of birth unknown, and six children.

In his will, Thomas is of Nether Wallop, Hampshire, England and refers to himself as a yeoman. His will indicates that Thomas was a prosperous farmer owning several buildings, over 200 sheep, cattle, and many debts were due him. Thomas requested to be buried in the churchyard of St. Andrews in Nether Wallop.

Thomas and Christian Kent's son Richard Kent was born about 1543. Apparently he was married twice, but the name of his first wife has not been found. In his will he refers to his "now wife" Elizabeth. Richard had two sons, Thomas and Richard, probably by his first wife. His will is dated 13 June 1609.

The existing records indicate that Richard was born and died in Nether Wallop, Hampshire, England.

Richard gave testimony in a court case in 1595 in which he described himself as a yeoman. Apparently, Richard was a prosperous yeoman as he was the only Kent from Nether Wallop who was taxed in the 1586 Hampshire Lay Subsidy and his will bequeathed a substantial amount of land to his children and other relatives.

During Richard's life time, England was mostly a protestant country.

St. Andrews Church, Nether Wallop, Hampshire, England

Richard's will requests that he be buried at the church of Nether Wallop which would be St. Andrews. Thomas Kent was born in Nether Wallop about 1563 to Richard and his first wife. He married Ellen Pyle, born 1554, in Over Wallop on 20 June 1585. The marriage produced nine children. Thomas preceded his father in death at Over Wallop, Hampshire, England on 25 May 1605. Ellen married Peter Osgood 17 February 1608.

In his will, Thomas refers to himself as a yeoman. He requested to be buried in the church or churchyard of Over Wallop, St. Peters.

St. Peter's Church, Over Wallop, Hampshire, England

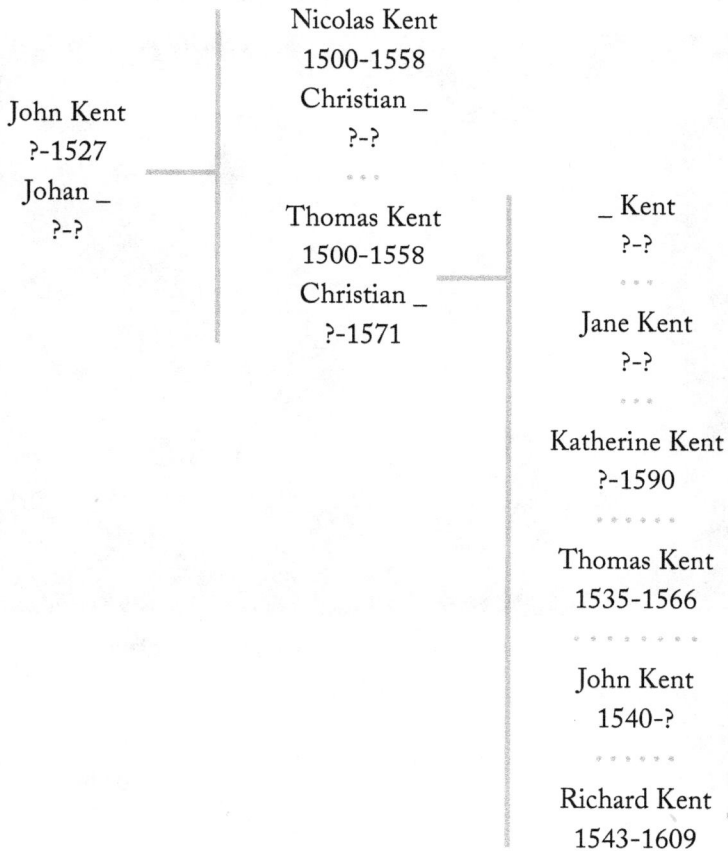

John Kent
?-1527
Johan _
?-?

Nicolas Kent
1500-1558
Christian _
?-?

Thomas Kent
1500-1558
Christian _
?-1571

_ Kent
?-?

Jane Kent
?-?

Katherine Kent
?-1590

Thomas Kent
1535-1566

John Kent
1540-?

Richard Kent
1543-1609

Richard Kent
1586-1654

Phillis Kent
1588-1588

Joanna Kent
1592-?

Thomas Kent
1594-1638

Martha Kent
1596-1638

David Kent
1598-1612

Mary Kent
1601-1629

John Kent
1603-1633

Thomas Kent
1563-1605

Ellen Pyle
1567-?

Stephen Kent
1605-1679

Richard Kent
1543-1609

Unknown

Richard Kent
1570-1638

The Kents and the Great Migration

Thomas and Ellen Kent had a son Thomas born about 1594 in Over Wallop, Hampshire, England. He married Maturnia whose last name is unknown. The couple had two children, Thomas and Mary.

Thomas' occupation is listed as clerk and he is said to have died in Over Wallop in 1638. He and his siblings broke with several generations of family tradition.

His brother Richard, born 1586, was a malster; he immigrated to the Massachusetts Bay Colony in 1633. His sister Martha, born 1596, married a minister educated at Oxford. Thomas's sister Mary was born in 1601 and died in 1629. Her widower husband, Nicholas Easton, immigrated to Massachusetts Bay Colony, was forced to leave the colony because of religious differences with the Puritans lead by John Winthrop, and moved to Rhode Island. There he became one of Rhode Island Colony's first governors. Thomas's brother John was attending Brasenose College at Oxford, England when he wrote his will in 1631. He said he was writing the will as he was going to travel, although he did not say where. He died in 1633 apparently without traveling. Thomas's brother Stephen, born 1605, was a linen draper. Stephen immigrated to the Massachusetts Bay Colony in 1638, but later moved to New Jersey Colony.[1]

Thomas Kent, born 1612, married Ann Noyes, born 1617, in England in 1631.[2] Ann was the daughter of Reverend William Noyes, a Puritan minister from Cholderton, Wiltshire, England. She had three brothers who were also Puritan ministers. Her brothers James and Nicholas Noyes arrived in 1634 in the Massachusetts Bay Colony. They were among the first Puritan ministers there. Her nephew, Nicholas Noyes, was the minister who presided at the hangings of alleged witches in the 1692 Salem Witch Trials.

Thomas and Ann immigrated to Gloucester, Massachusetts Bay

Colony about 1640.[3] There seems to be no record as to whether or not Thomas and Ann were accompanied by servants as some of their relatives were. At least two of their relations had Negro slaves. In his will, Richard Kent Jr. freed "Cussa a negro man."[4] Samuel Kent Jr. of Suffield sold an eight or nine year old slave named Kate for £89 in 1734.[5] Other relatives arrived in New England with servants who might have been indentured.[6]

Thomas owned land in Gloucester by 1643. His occupation is listed as farmer.[7] Thomas died in Gloucester 1 May 1658.[8] His widow lived until 16 October 1671.[9] Their children, all born in England, were Thomas, Samuel, and Josiah.

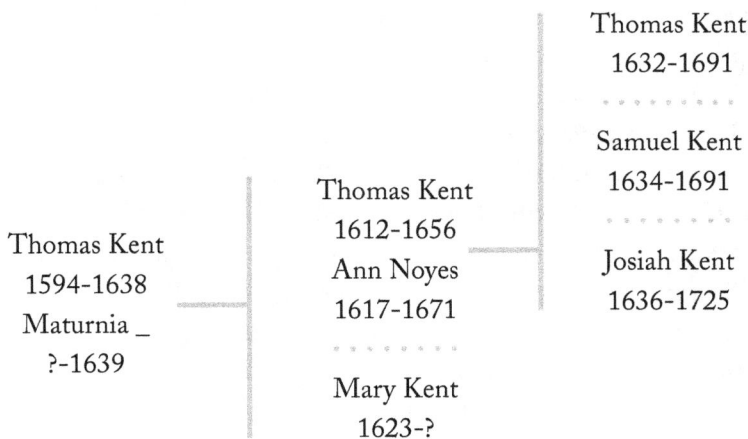

Thomas Kent
1594-1638
Maturnia _
?-1639

Thomas Kent
1612-1656
Ann Noyes
1617-1671

Mary Kent
1623-?

Thomas Kent
1632-1691

Samuel Kent
1634-1691

Josiah Kent
1636-1725

The Kents and the Indian Wars

Samuel Kent was born in England in 1634.[10] He immigrated to Gloucester, Massachusetts Bay Colony with his parents and two brothers in 1640, at the age of six. Both his younger and older brothers were born in Over Wallop, Hampshire, England but records say that Samuel was born in Essex, England.[11] At the age of twenty, on 17 January 1654, Samuel married Frances Woodall, born 1636, in Gloucester, Massachusetts Bay Colony.[12] They had four children, all born in Gloucester.

In 1671, Samuel and his brother Thomas left Gloucester and moved their families southwest to Quaboag Plantation in the Massachusetts Bay Colony. At the time Samuel's daughter Sarah was fourteen, Mary was thirteen, Samuel was ten, and John was seven. Samuel and his brother Thomas bought land at the plantation. Quaboag Plantation became an incorporated township known as Brookefeild [sic] in 1673. It is not possible to determine whether Samuel acquired the title Sargent as part of the militia at Quaboag/Brookfield or later on. During the summer of 1675 tensions between the English settlers and some of the Native Americans in New England became very strained. These two groups were competing for land and other resources. Metacom, a Wampanoag chief, who called himself King Philip, began attacking English settlements in June of 1675. On August second, Nipmuck natives attacked Brookfield. The Brookfield inhabitants took shelter in Ayres Tavern. The Native American siege lasted until August fourth when English troops arrived. Most of the town was burned during the siege. Apparently all of Samuel's family survived, as none of the Kents are listed among the dead after the siege[13]. Thomas Kent returned to Gloucester with his family and possibly Samuel and family did too.

By 1676 Samuel was granted 60 acres of land in Suffield, Massachusetts Bay Colony which later would become a part of Connecticut Colony.

Samuel's grant was the first to be given after Suffield was completely burned during King Philip's War.[14] Samuel received two more grants of land at Suffield and was active in town affairs.

On 27 September 1681 Samuel took his oath as a freeman of the colony.[15] 1686 Court records contain the following:

"Samuel Kent of Suffield having been bound over to this Court for raising and abetting a mutiny and riotous behavior at Suffield, and himself very much active in such carriages, besides several unworthy speeches, as in a high and violent manner, saying, that all persons might vote at the town meeting, in choice of townsmen, and constable, etc., That the laws of the government some of them were not worth a chip, and being present when there was a tumult and disorder in the town meeting, abetting said non-voters saying they might vote, with offense and evil carriages and speeches. This Court judge high abusive carriages, tending to breaking of order, and in reality breach of order, in reality a breach of law, and grievous violations of his religious tye, which is upon him, have adjudged the said Kent to pay as fine to the county treasurer, the full sum of 5 pounds and charges of witnesses and other wise, and the money to pay forthwith, or to give good security"[16]

Sargent Samuel Kent died at Springfield Massachusetts Bay Colony 2 February 1691. His wife, Frances passed eight years before him on 10 August 1683 in Suffield.

Daughter Sarah married Richard Coy Jr. Little is known about daughter Mary. The sons Samuel and John remained in Suffield their entire lives raising large families and were very active in the affairs of the settlement.

Sarah Kent
1657-1724

Mary Kent
1658-?

Samuel Kent
1634-1691
Frances Woodall
1636-1683

Samuel Kent Jr.
1661-1740

John Kent
1664-1721

The Kents After King Philip's War

"The effects of the war, on both the colonists and the natives, were disastrous. By the end of the war, more than 600 colonists had died, around 1,200 homes had been burned and around 12 out of 90 new settlements were destroyed.

The wide scale destruction caused such devastating financial losses the English expansion in the region completely stopped for 50 years.

The losses were far worse for the natives though. Out of the total population of 20,000 Native-Americans in southern New England at the time, an estimated 2,000 were killed, another 3,000 had died of sickness and starvation, around 1,000 were captured and sold into slavery, and an estimated 2,000 fled to join the Iroquois in the west or the Abenaki in the north. This adds up to a loss of between 60 to 80 percent of the native population in the region.

The war also ruined New England's economy by nearly halting the fur trade, killing 8,000 head of cattle, interrupting the importing and exporting of goods and causing a decline in the fishing industry. In addition, wartime expenses of around 80,000 pounds led to high taxes."[17]

Despite the effects of the war, John Kent and his brother Samuel seemed to have thrived. In April of 1685 John leased land in Suffield from John Pynchon of the prosperous and legendary Pynchon family. By the following year he had married Abigail Dudley and by 1687 became the father of the first of his twelve children. With Abigail Dudley, John had the following children: Mary, John, Abigail, Deborah, Dudley, Mary, Samuel, Abner and Elisha. Abigail Dudley died three months after Elisha was born, on 26 October 1704. On 19 May 1709 John married Abigail Winchell. Together they had three children: Joseph, Noah, and Experience.[18] Captain John served as Clerk of the Band for the Suffield Militia and as Representative of Suffield in the General Court for many years.[19]

Captain John Kent's son Elisha graduated from Yale College as a minister in 1729. In 1732 he married Abigail Moss and was elected as minister in Newtown, Connecticut Colony. Elisha's son Moss graduated from Yale in 1752 and was admitted to the bar of New York in 1755. In addition to practicing law he became a judge.[20] Moss's son James Kent was born 31 July 1763 and died 12 December 1847.

Chancellor James Kent

"It is a remarkable coincidence of events that while we are engaged in recording the death of the distinguished author of the "Commentaries on American Law," at an age seldom allotted to man, the telegraph should be announcing that the mortal career of his eminent and far-famed colleague, Judge SPENCER, is near its close, and the sands of life ebbing fast. Both had filled, for many years, the high office of Chief Justice of this State, and exercised a powerful and an abiding influence on its public concerns; both had reached the advanced age of fourscore and beyond it, retaining in full vigor their highly cultivated mental powers; and it would seem that like the remarkable concurrence in the time of the demise of President Adams and Jefferson, Judges KENT and SPENCER are, nearly together, to leave a world which they benefitted and adorned, for that blessed immortality which is the Christisn's hope while on earth and his reward through eternity.

JAMES KENT was born on the 31st of July, 1763, in Fredericksburg, then part of Dutchess, but now of Putnam County, New York, and was the eldest son of Moss Kent, a graduate of Yale College, Connecticut, who was admitted to the Bar of Dutchess County in 1756. His grandfather, Rev. Elisha Kent, a native of Suffield, Conn., was for thirty-six years minister of the Presbyterian Congregation of Kent Parish in Dutchess County, and his brother, Moss, sat in the Senate of this State, and in

Congress, and was for some time Register of the Court of Chancery.

Mr. KENT was sent to school at Norwalk when but five years old, and was placed under various instructors until he entered Yale College in September, 1777, more than 70 years since. From the precepts, and yet more the example, of those pious Puritans among whom his early years were passed he acquired that simplicity of character and purity of morals which he preserved through life.

In July, 1779, New-Haven was invaded by the British forces, the College broken up and the students dispersed. In his exile, young Kent met with Blackstone's Commentaries, read, admired, and, at sixteen, determined to be a lawyer, he finally left college with high reputation, studied law with Egbert Benson, Attorney-General of New-York, was studious, temperate and a water-drinker, indulging in none of the fashionable pleasures or dissipation of the times. An enthusiastic admirer of Nature's charms, the love of reading was his ruling passion. He was cheerful, lively and communicative—young, ardent, active and persevering—his mind was early stored with useful knowledge, and the morning of his life gave promise of the noonday brilliancy of his remarkable career.

In April, 1787, he was admitted, at Albany, a Counselor of the Supreme Court—in 1790, and again in 1792, elected to the Legislature by the people of his native county. From the purest motives, and believing its policy the best for his country, he joined the Federal party, became the steadfast friend of Jay, Hamilton and others of its leaders, to whose political principles and usages he steadily adhered, until, in 1819, it ceased to exist.

After failing to be elected to Congress by a few votes, he removed, in 1793, from Poughkeepsie to this City, was appointed Professor of Law in Columbia College, and delivered a course of lectures the year following. In 1796 he was appointed a Master in Chancery—there were then but two of them, and next year called to fill the office of Recorder of New York. In 1798 he ascended the Supreme Court bench as one of the Judges, and removed his residence to Albany, where he commenced the practice of delivering a written, augmentative opinion, supported by legal authorities, in every case of sufficient importance to become a precedent for the future. Thus commenced that series of recorded judicial decisions which have enriched the jurisprudence of New York, and proved alike useful to the legislator, the judge, and the codifier.

Judges KENT and RAINCLIFFE revised the Statues of our State in 1800. In July, 1804, the former was appointed Chief Justice of the State, and continued to preside in the Supreme Court until his appointment as Chancellor of Feb., 1814. His legal opinions, delivered while in the Supreme Court, are contained in 16 volumes of well-known and highly appreciated reports.

As Chancellor, which high office he filled till 1823, he is understood to have displayed to great advantage these excellent business habits and that promptitude which marked his career through a long and invaluable life. A few favored lawyers had, before his time, monopolized Chancery business—he threw its doors wide open to the profession—and was un- wearied in his efforts to dispatch the causes brought under his cognizance.

By the Constitution of 1821, the Judges were removable from office at 60 years of age; and, on July 31, 1823, he, having reached that period, retired, after bearing and carefully deciding every case that had been brought before him. The members of the bar in this City and Albany took that occasion to bear ample testimony to his worth and usefulness, and to acknowledge the benefits which society had derived from his learning, wisdom and assiduity. In 1824, he became a second time Law Professor in Columbia College, and in 1826 appeared the first volume of his in- estimable 'Commentaries on American Law,' which were concluded in four volumes in 1830, and have been extended and improved by him, with great care, from that period to this.

Chancellor KENT would not allow his Commentaries to be ste- reotyped, but kept watching the decisions of the tribunals of America, England, and other parts of Europe, in matters involving important legal principles, with which be enriched his favorite work from time to time.

He was elected President of the New York Historical Society in 1828, and was an original member of the Literary Association of Yale College, formed in 1780, under the name of the Phi Beta Kappa Society. In 1821, he represented Albany County in the State Constitutional Convention, AMBROSE SPENCER now on his death bed, being his colleague. He was a distinguished ornament of that learned and patriotic body, and steadily adhered to the opinion that with a constituency of freeholders, owners and cultivators of the soil, the unencumbered possessors of happy homesteads, the liberties of the country would be safest. In 1785, be [sic] married a sister of Gen. THEODORSUS BAILEY, a lady now nearly 80 years old, and who survives him, after enjoying over three score years of uninterrupted domestic felicity. His family consisted of two daughters and one son, the learned and well-known Judge KENT, who resigned the office of Circuit Judge here some years since, and more recently gave up his Professorship at Cambridge that he might cheer the latter days of his venerated and excellent father by his company and personal attentions.

Our neighbor of the Express states, that less than a year ago, Chancellor Kent was one of the pallbearers of his friend, TIMOTHY DWIGHT, and was then as erect, hale and active as a man of fifty. At 84, he was somewhat deaf, but his capacity for work was still wonderful, his conversation interesting and animated, and his temperament as vivacious as when he was thirty years younger. He was unwell but for a short time before his death, which took place last Sunday evening at half past eight, at his residence in Union-square. The Courts adjourned yesterday out of respect for his memory, and both Boards of the Common Council adopted resolutions in honor of his name and character.

He was an exemplary Christian, a steadfast and affectionate father, a tender husband, an ardent patriot, and a true lover and defender of his country's rights. So highly are his works esteemed abroad that the Lord Chief Justice of England, Baron DERMAN, wrote to Judge KENT, some years since, to acknowledge the indebtedness of the legal profession throughout the world to him for his able commentaries.

The remains of Chancellor KENT are to be interred tomorrow (Wednesday.) The services will be performed at the Cavalry church, Fourth avenue.—The funeral procession will leave his house at half-past three in the afternoon, and we agree with the Commercial, where it expresses a belief "that a longer procession, or one more strikingly representing the intelligence and the high character in every respect, of our community, has never been seen following the hearse of a private citizen, than will be that which follows to its resting place the body of the venerable and illustrious JAMES KENT."[21]

Mary Kent
1687-1688

John Kent
1688-1737

Abigail Kent
1690-1767

Deborah Kent
1693-1773

John Kent
1664-1721
Abigail Dudley
1667-1709

Dudley Kent
1695-1766

Mary Kent
1697-?

Samuel Kent
1698-1772

Abner Kent
1701-1776

Elisha Kent
1704-1776

Joseph Kent
1710-1753

John Kent
1664-1721
Abigail Winchell
1679-1767

Noah Kent
1714-1755

Experience Kent
1717-1795

The Kents before the
French and Indian War

Captain John Kent and his second wife Abigail's son, Noah, was born 28 April 1714 in Suffield, Massachusetts Bay Colony. His father passed away when Noah was six. At the age of twenty, in 1734, Noah married Deliverance Granger whose grandfather, like Noah's, was a first settler and land grantee in Suffield, Massachusetts Bay Colony.[22] At that time the First Great Awakening, a series of Christian revivals, was sweeping through the British Colonies. Suffield became part of Connecticut in 1749 correcting a surveying error from its earliest settlement. Noah and Deliverance had nine children between 1735 and 1755. Noah passed away 25 May 1755. Deliverance had her ninth child on the 1 December 1755 and she passed away on 25 December 1755 just as the French and Indian War was beginning.

Phoebe Kent
1735-1762

Noah Kent
1737-1812

Gideon Kent
1739-?

Daniel Kent
1747-1750

Noah Kent
1714-1755
Deliverance Granger
1713-1755

Deborah Kent
1748-1813

Mary Kent
1750-?

Nathaniel Kent
1751-1810

Abel Kent
1753-1807

Deliverance Kent
1755-1814

The Kents During the French and Indian War and the American Revolution

Noah Kent born 27 August 1737 was seventeen when his father died and had recently turned eighteen when his mother passed.

In 1754 and 1755 the French and their Native American allies became increasingly at odds with the British over which parts of northern North America belonged to whom. By 1756 the British officially declared war.[23] Noah and his brother, Gideon, both served in the war. Phineas Lyman was the Regiment Commander of all Connecticut forces that fought in the war. In 1756 Noah's Company Commander was his uncle, Captain Aaron Hitchcock. When Noah served in the war in 1758 and 1759, his Company Commander was Phineas Lyman, considered an exceptional military officer. Noah's rank in 1758 was corporal; in 1759 it was sergeant.[24]

By 1762, Noah had settled in the new settlement of Lanesborough, Massachusetts Bay Colony where he purchased land on October 4, 1762.[25] In 1763 Noah married Lois Warren of Lanesborough. They continued to reside in Lanesborough through the birth of all of Noah's eleven children. Apparently Noah's brothers Able and Gideon also moved to Lanesborough.[26] In 1765, about a month after his first child was born; Noah and his brother Able were involved in the Lanesborough Affair.

"The Colonies in 1765

The Lanesborough Affair was an incident that occurred on 1765. This incident involved the entire town of Lanesborough. It occurred 10 years before the first shot of the American Revolution, however, it is a perfect example of the growing unhappiness of the colonists with the King. The incident was a result of the stamp act of 1765. Before we can tell the story the "Lanesborough Affair" we need to provide a brief overview of the stamp act as it pertains to our story.

The Stamp Act

The stamp act required a stamped paper produced in London be used for all paper products such as newspapers, magazines and all legal documents. Land, imported products would all have to possess a stamp before it could be purchased. There were several problems with this tax. The colonists considered this a violation of their rights as English subjects who in paying this tax had no representatives in Parliament, therefore had no voice in how this tax was spent. The famous quote "No taxation without representation" was born out of the stamp act. Another problem was the tax had to be paid in British currency and not currency of the colonies. Most colonists had no access to British currency. This created problems resulting in debts of the colonists. The fact that a stamp had to be affixed to all legal documents which included writs or warrants for arrest and court documents played a key role in the "Lanesborough Affair". In Berkshire County this stamped paper was simply not available. The people were unable mostly to purchase products that were imported because they were unable to pay the British tax (in British currency). This created debts which could not be paid. Protests took place throughout the colonies. The stamp act was short lived. Instituted on November 1, 1765 it was repealed the following March.

People Involved

The whole town was involved and stood together as one to prevent arrests. However, some people were more involved than others and as a result were arrested. The primary players in the situation were Peter Curtis who was on the list of Lanesborough's first settlers and John Franklin. These 2 men are who the sheriff came to arrest for having unpaid debts. The sheriff was Elijah Williams and his deputy sheriff was John Morse. Other members of the sheriff's party were Thomas Williams of Stockbridge, Eli Root, Elith Jones, Samuel Warner and a man referred to only as Captain Lord. Men arrested for their participation in the incident were Noah, Gideon and Abel Kent, James Loomis Jr., Seth Warren, Samuel Dorwin Jr., David Wheeler, Ichabod Hickok and of course Peter Curtis and John Franklin.

What Happened?
November 6, 1765

There were 2 towns people who had debt that could not be paid. They were John Franklin and Peter Curtis. Because of the new Stamp Act they knew, if a stamp was not affixed to the writs for arrest, it would not be a lawful arrest. They probably also knew, no such stamps were available in Berkshire County. Everyone in Lanesborough knew the circumstances and knew it was possible the sheriff would be coming to Lanesborough to make arrests. They also knew that because of new policies, once arrested, the prisoners would have no rights and be unable to obtain any sort of bond. They could be imprisoned indefinitely with no legal recourse. On the morning of November 6, 1765 the townspeople had gathered together for a house raising. The subject was discussed and everyone agreed that if the sheriff came to town to make arrests, they would not permit it until the King's writ (with the stamp) could be secured. This would allow the prisoners their legal rights. That same evening Sheriff Morse entered the tavern in Lanesborough holding 2 writs for arrest of John Franklin and Peter Curtis. The writs did not contain a stamp, therefore were not legal under the new stamp act. What occurred next has been described in detail by Joseph Hawley an attorney (and true patriot) from Northampton and published in the Boston Evening Post in 1766. Anything written in quotes is his account as published.

Sheriff Morse entered Lanesborough accompanied by 5 other men Capt. Lord, Mess. Elith Jones, Samuel Warner, Thomas Williams and Eli Root with a writ to arrest Peter Curtis. The group entered the tavern in Lanesborough and Elisha Jones arrested Peter Curtis with these words: "Now Fatler [sic]Peter you old devil I have got you and you shall go to goal" Morse then saw John Franklin who he also had an arrest warrant for. Sheriff Morse commanded the townspeople in the tavern to grab him. It was at this point the sheriff realized the townspeople were not happy. In the meantime, Joseph Loomis had slipped out of the tavern and went next door to the house of Noah Kent. He told Noah what was happening and the 2 men returned to the tavern. As Noah entered the tavern, he saw his younger brother Abel Kent on the floor of the tavern with Mr. Jones on top of him. Abel had attempted to release Peter Curtis from the grip of Elisha Jones. What happened next I will quote Jospeh [sic] Hawley's words. "Upon Noah Kent's seeing his brother Abel down, and restrained by Jones in manner aforesaid, he rescued Abel and encountered Jones, Threw him on the floor, fell on him, held him down for a minute or two, then suffered him to get up." After this, words were exchanged, some profane and Morse's party got physical and attacked. The only man of Morse's group who did not participate in the brawl was Captain Lord. When things calmed down, the Lanesborough men according to Joseph Hawley's account remained calm and tried to explain their concerns. They tried to engage Morse in a conversation hoping he would listen to reason, however, Morse would not engage in such conversation and insisted on executing his writ. When the Lanesborough men realized he would not listen to their concerns that his writ was not legal, they let him know he would not be making any arrests that day. The men were forced out of the tavern and the crowd threw rocks at them until they left. It should be noted no one was actually hit by the rocks. Later, ten of the men involved in this incident were arrested for their participation. Among those arrested and charged with unlawful assembly and riot were Seth Warren, Noah Kent and Abel Kent. Seth Warren was the only man of the 10 to plea not guilty to the charges. He hired Northampton attorney Joseph Hawley to represent him. Joseph Hawley wrote an article that was published in the Boston Evening Post regarding this incident."[27] In Joseph Hawley's article, he refers to all three Kents as yeomen.[28]

Noah had five children before he first served, with three of his brothers, as a Minuteman in the American Revolution. Although Noah continued to reside in Lanesborough at that time, his brothers Gideon, Able, and Nathaniel were living in New Ashford, Massachusetts Bay Colony just a few miles away.

On April 22, 1775 Noah entered service as a Minuteman in response to the opening battle of the Revolutionary War at Lexington and Concord, Massachusetts Bay Colony. On December 8, 1776 he participated in the last campaign of that year when he marched from Rehoboth, Massachusetts Bay Colony to Bristol, Rhode Island Colony when the British captured Newport, Rhode Island Colony. On August 4, 1777 Noah march to Walloomsac, New York Colony to participate in what became called the Battle of Bennington, Vermont. Finally twice in October of 1780 he marched to a place called "the Northward." The Northward was probably that area north of the Massachusetts Bay Colony claimed by both New Hampshire Colony and New York Colony. He spent a total of fifty-seven days in Revolutionary War service returning to his farm and family when not acting as a soldier. [29]

Noah's wife Lois had their last child in 1787. There seems to be no record of her death. By 1792 Noah was in Utica, New York which was now a state. He signed a petition to the state legislature on October 24, 1792 requesting funds to build a bridge.[30] According to New York tax assessment rolls, Noah had a house and farm in Rome, New York in 1800 valued at $365.00.[31] In 1812, at age seventy-four, Noah died in Rome, New York.

Asa Kent
1765-?

Eli Kent
1767-1822

Noah Kent Jr.
1769-?

Warren Kent
1771-1839

Anna Kent
1773-?

Noah Kent
1737-1812
Lois Warren
1746-?

Lois Kent
1775-1857

Carrel Kent
1777-1860

Mary Kent
1779-?

David Kent
1782-?

Elijah Kent
1784-1822

Joseph Kent
1787-1828

The Kents and the War of 1812

Eli Kent was born 23 April 1767 in Lanesborough, Massachusetts Bay Colony. His formative years would have been heavily influenced by events leading up to the American Revolution and the Revolution itself. At age nineteen, Eli married Anna Lyons on 5 January 1787 in Pittsfield which is just south of Lanesborough. His first two children were born in Massachusetts. Apparently he followed his father to the Rome area of New York in 1795 and farmed there.[32] The rest of his six children were born in New York.

Eli served twice in the War of 1812. He first served in Captain Joel B. Clark's Company, Colonel Philetus Swift's Regiment from 9 September to 15 December 1813. Secondly, he served in Capitan Issac Curtis's Company, Colonel D. Roger 1's Regiment from 8 September 1814 to 11 December 1814.[33] Eli's son-in-law, Benjamin Gardner husband of Lois Kent, also served in the War of 1812. Benjamin served at the large naval base in Sackett's Harbor, New York on Lake Ontario.

Eli and his children seemed to have survived the 1816 "Year Without a Summer." He died in 1822 and was buried near his farm in Rome, New York. Anna died in 1844, but her place of death is not mentioned.

Nathaniel Kent
1787-1876

Lois Kent
1789-1880

Orrin Kent
1796-1863

Eli Kent
1767-1822
Anna Lyons
1767-1844

Samuel Kent
1800-1880

Rueben Carrel Kent
1802-1875

Joseph Kent
1805-?

The Kents and Westward Expansion

Eli Kent's son Orrin also served in the War of 1812. He was eighteen years of age when he was paid for service from 22 August 1814 to 16 November 1814.[34]

By 1820 Orrin was married to Mary Conde, who was born in 1805 in New York, and his first child, Orin Samuel Kent, was born. The first nine of his ten children were born in the Rome area of New York.

On 1 May 1845 Orrin was granted 40 acres of land in Lake County, Illinois.[35] On 5 September 1845 he purchased 80 acres of land in the same area.[36] On 1 June 1846 he was granted 80 acres of land in Lake County, Illinois.[37]

Orrin Kent's tenth child, Lydia Ann, was born in 1846 in Illinois. All nine of her siblings moved west from New York to frontier territory at some point in their lives. Horace Ayrault Kent listed his occupation as miner in El Dorado California during the California Gold Rush.[38] By 1853 Horace was living in Oregon working as a merchant.[39] By 1850 Arba Kent was working as a laborer in Michigan.[40] Fredrick G. Kent married Amanda Mead on 4 July 1851 in Lake County, Illinois.[41] They were both living in Newport, Lake County, Illinois in 1900.[42] Darius Aloak, Mary, Eli Pelig, Betsy Ann, and John W. all came to Illinois with their parents.[43] By the time he served in the Civil War, Darius was living in Michigan where he died.[44] Mary married and had her only child in Michigan.[45] Eli Pelig was also living in Michigan by the age of twenty-two.[46] Betsy Ann and John W. both died in Michigan.[47]

Orrin died 16 December 1863 in Warren, Lake County, Illinois two years after Abraham Lincoln, who was also from Illinois, became president and the Civil War began. Apparently he left no will.[48] His wife received four hundred dollars in the probate case. Mary Conde passed away 21 November 1866 in Muskegon, Michigan where her son John W. and daughter Lydia lived.

Orin Samuel Kent
1820-?

· · · · · ·

Horace A. Kent
1821-1859

· · · · · · · ·

Fredrick G. Kent
1824-1900

· · · · · · · ·

Arba B. Kent
1824-1917

· · · · · · · ·

Orrin Kent
1796-1863
Mary Conde
1805-1866

Darius A. Kent
1830-1876

· · · · · · · ·

Mary Kent
1834-1857

· · · · · · · ·

Eli P. Kent
1838-1899

· · · · · · · ·

Betsy Ann Kent
1841-1911

· · · · · · · ·

John W. Kent
1843-1885

· · · · · · · ·

Lydia Ann Kent
1846-1918

The Kents Continue Westward

Orin Samuel Kent, born in 1820, grew up in the Rome/Floyd area of New York.[49] At age twenty he married his first cousin Elizabeth Ann Betsy Gardner.[50] She was the daughter of Orin Samuel's father's sister Lois Kent and her husband Benjamin Gardner. Elizabeth was nineteen at the time of her marriage. In 1841 their son Albert B. Kent was born.[51] Elizabeth died in 1844 when her son was only three years old.[52] After the death of his wife, Orin Samuel moved to Sylvester, Green County, Wisconsin about one hundred miles northwest of where his father was living in Warren, Lake County, Illinois. He left Albert B. to be raised by his grandparents Benjamin and Lois Gardner in Floyd, Oneida County, New York.[53] In 1845, Orin Samuel married Catherine Warner.[54] They had two children, Charles Arby and Mary E., both born in Wisconsin.[55] By 1887 Charles Arby was living in Columbia Territory which would become the state Of Washington in 1889.[56] A Washington Select Death Certificate lists the death of Samuel Kent, Spouse Warner, Child Charles Arby, and Household Members Warner, Samuel Kent, Charles Arby Kent, Sarah R. Ray. There is no date on the certificate.[57]

Orin Samuel Kent
1820-?
Elizabeth Ann Betsy Gardner
1821-1844

Albert B. Kent
1841-1870

Orin Samuel Kent
1820-?
Catherine Warner
1824-?

Charles Arby Kent
1848-1920

Mary E. Kent
1850-?

The Kents and the Civil War

Albert B. Kent was living with his grandparents, farmer Benjamin and Lois Gardner and his aunt Harriet P. Gardner in August of 1850 when he was listed on the federal census as being eight years old.[58] At that time Harriet was 26 and probably acted as a substitute mother for Albert as she was listed on Kent family notes.[59] By the time Albert was 19, he was living in Binghamton, Broom County, New York working as a clerk.[60] On 27 October 1861 Albert enlisted as a private in the Union Army at Camp Treadway, Janesville, Wisconsin in the 13th Infantry Regiment, Company K.[61] Janesville, Wisconsin was about thirty miles east of where Albert's father, Orin Samuel, was living in Sylvester, Greene County, Wisconsin with his second wife and two young children at that time.

"The 13th Wisconsin Infantry was organized at Camp Tredway in Janesville and mustered into service on October 17, 1861. The regiment left Wisconsin for Leavenworth, Kansas, on January 13, 1862. During its service it moved through Missouri, Kentucky, Alabama, and Tennessee, where it served on duty at Forts Henry and Donelson. The regiment mustered out on November 24, 1865, having lost 193 men. Five enlisted men were killed and 188 enlisted men died from disease."[62]

Albert was honorably discharged from the 13th Infantry 18 May 1862 at Fort Riley, Kansas having developed kidney disease.[63] In June of 1663 he was living in Leyden, New York listed as a workman. Apparently Albert worked on the railroad that ran through Potsdam, New York where he met his future wife, Jane Brewer.[64] They were married 31 March 1864.[65] Their son Charles Orin was born in 1866, Albert John was born 1867, and daughter Elizabeth "Libbie" "Nellie" was born in 1869. Albert died of kidney failure in April of 1870 leaving Jane and her three children living with Jane's parents in Potsdam, NY.[66] On 22 May of 1870 Jane had Albert John and "Libbie "baptized at St. Mary's Catholic

Church in Potsdam. Charles Orin was probably also baptized there that day, but he baptism certificate is not found.[67] Prior to this it is believed that the Kent family had been Methodist Episcopalians.

In May of 1876 Jane, originally French Canadian married Peter Counter, also French Canadian. Peter had only been in the United States

Seven members of the 13th Wisconsin Volunteer Infantry Company K.
Albert B. Kent is not among these men, but they were his fellow soldiers.[74]

for two years at that time.[68] Their daughter Mary was born in 1878 and their son Joseph was born in 1879. Apparently they had two more children.[69] According to Kent family notes, all the Counter children died of diphtheria.[70] Jane and Peter were living with her daughter Elizabeth and her husband Herbert Halford when Peter died 19 July 1910.[71] Jane was working as a laundress in 1915 and still living with the Halfords. [72] By 1919 Jane was living at 38 Maple Street in Potsdam, New York with her son Charles O. Kent. She died 3 December 1920 at age seventy-four.[73]

Jane Brewer

Jane's Second Husband
Peter Counter

Albert B. Kent
1841-1870
Jane Brewer
1846-1920

Charles O. Kent
1866-1927

. . . .

Albert John "Johnny" Kent
1867-1948

. . . .

Elizabeth "Libbie" "Nellie" Kent
1869-1954

The Kents During Reconstruction and World War I

Charles Orin Kent was four years old when his father died. By 1880 Charles and his brother Albert John, who apparently went by Johnny later in life, were working in a saw mill.[75] Charles would have been fourteen at the time and Johnny was only twelve. Their stepfather, Peter, was working in a talc mill. The family had relocated from Potsdam, New York to Gouverneur, New York. At some point Charles and Johnny joined the W.W. Cole's New Colossal Shows, a circus which was established in 1884.[76]

By 1889 Charles was back in Potsdam when he married Minnie May DeGof.[77] Minnie is listed as Minnie Perrin on some documents, but she was never legally adopted by the Perrin family.[78] Minnie's biological father was said to be a Dr. DeGoeff or Dr. DeGoss who came from England.[79] There was a Marth DeGof who arrived in the United States from England in 1867 at age twenty-five.[80] Minnie was born in April of 1871. Apparently Minnie's mother died when Minnie was about three. Her father began drinking heavily and died soon after. By 1880 Minnie was living with the Perrin family in Potsdam, New York and going by their last name.

Charles and Minnie's first child, Albert Byron Kent, was born 3 September 1890 in Augusta, Maine.[81] By 1900 Charles, Minnie and Albert were living at 42 1/2 Maple Street in Potsdam, New York. Charles' mother and step-father were living with them.[82] Charles was working as a machinist by then. On 10 February 1895 their daughter Margret was born; she lived less than a year, dying on 12 August 1895[83]. Charles O. Kent Jr. was born 10 February 1905[84]. Charles Senior did not serve in World War I as he had a dependent spouse and dependent child under sixteen in 1917. He continued working as a machinist in Potsdam until shortly before he died on 27 January 1927.

"Charles 0. Kent, life time resident of Potsdam, died at his home on Maple street, Thursday, January 27. He had been in poor health for a long time but was not confined to the trade. He secured employment in the house until very recently. Mr. Kent was born here April 28, 1866, son of Albert and Jane Kent. He attended the local schools and at an early age learned the machinist's Leete foundry and was a faithful and trusted employe [sic] there for over thirty years. His father worked in the same shop before him. Mr. Kent married Miss Minne [sic] Perrin and two sons were born to them, Albert of Syracuse and Charles of this place. Mrs. Kent and the two sons survive besides one sister, Mrs. Herbert Halford of Potsdam. Funeral services were held at St. Mary's church Saturday with interment at St Mary's cemetery."[85]

Charles O. Kent at Lette's Machine Shop on Fall Island in Potsdam, New York. Charles is the person balanced on the equipment in the middle of the photo.

Minnie M. DeGof

Charles O. Kent
1866-1927
Minnie M. DeGof
1871-1957

Albert Byron Kent
1890-1950
. . . .
Margret Kent
1895-1895
. . . .
Charles O. Kent Jr.
1905-1970

The Kents and Prohibition, the Great Depression and World War II

It remains a mystery why Albert Byron Kent was born in Augusta, Maine as both of his parents were from Potsdam, New York and that is where they were married. Apparently he attended school as a young man as he was able to read and write. At age twenty, he was working as a house painter.[86] On 29 January 1913, Albert married Katherine N. Gardner of Gouverneur, New York. At the time of his marriage, Albert was working as a brush maker.[87]

"A quiet home wedding took place at 2 P. M. last Wednesday at the home of Mr. and Mrs. Joseph Gardner in Parker Street when their youngest daughter, Miss Katie Newcomb Gardner, became the bride of Albert Byron Kent, a popular young Potsdam man. The ceremony was performed by Rev. James A. Dickson, rector of Trinity Episcopal Church in the presence of a good number of relatives and friends of the young couple, several being present from Potsdam. At the completion of the ceremony light refreshments were served after which the young couple left on the 4:26 west bound train for Watertown where they have been spending several days as guests of relatives and friends. They will reside in Potsdam."[88]

On 16 December 1913 their first child, Orin Nelson, was born in Gouverneur, New York.[89] By 1915, Albert, Kate and Orin were living with Charles, Minnie, and Charles Jr. on Maple Street in Potsdam, New York and Albert was still working at the brush factory. Albert registered for the first World War I draft on June 5, 1917 while working as a tool maker in Watertown, New York. He was exempted as he had a wife and dependent child under sixteen.[90] Between 1917 and 1920 Albert and his wife and son had moved to Syracuse, New York where their second son, Sterling Albert, was born 1 March 1920. They were still living in Syracuse in 1925 where Albert was working as a tool maker when his

Orin and Sterling Kent Miami Beach, 1942

third child, Alberta Jane, was born on 29 November.[91] During Prohibition, beginning in 1920 and lasting until 1933, when manufacture, transportation and sale of alcohol was prohibited, Kate recalled she and Albert hiding liquor in the baby's carriage on weekends and walking to visit friends.[92]

Albert's father died in 1927 and the Great Depression began in 1929. Whether it was for those reasons or some other, by 1930 Albert and Katherine had moved back to Potsdam, NY and were living with Minnie Kent at 38 Maple Street with their three children. Minnie also had three boarders at the time, one of whom was Katherine's father, Joseph Nelson Gardner, whose wife had died in 1925.[93]

In January and February of 1938, Albert and Katherine purchased the house at forty-two Maple Street in Potsdam from Albert's aunt, Elizabeth "Nellie" Kent. At the time Elizabeth and her husband, Herbert Halford, were separated and divorcing. In the legal agreement, Albert and Katherine consented to provide Elizabeth with room, board, medical care, and a respectable burial.[94] Now they were a family of seven as Katherine's father had been living with them since 1935. However, Joseph Nelson Gardner passed away on December 13, 1938.[95]

Albert's uncle Johnny, Albert John Kent, came to live with Albert and Katherine in 1941, so again the household was back to seven members.

As was required by law, Albert registered for the World War II draft on April 26, 1942. At the time he was working at the Aluminum Company of America in Massena, New York.[96] He was too old to serve. However his son Orin was drafted and his son Sterling enlisted. According to a

12/21/42

Dear Brother + Sister

I am sending you a picture of Quin and Sterling taken at Miami Beach, Fla. Sterling inlisted and left ~~March~~ 2 and is a sergeant now stationed at MacDill Fla. Had a letter from him this morning saying he was going to be sent to Lakeland Fla. this week. He is a crew chief and repairs the air planes or the ground. Quin was drafted and left Sept 9th and is 1-B- limited~~to all~~ service stationed in the Finance Dept at Miami Beach, Fla. Quin's wife is going to Florida Jan 1- to stay. It doesn't seem much like Xmas to us this year with the boys gone. I guess Albert will never get over it.

Kate

note written on the back of a photograph of Kate's military sons sent to family members in December of 1942, Albert was distraught over his sons leaving for war.[97]

Sterling entered World War II service in March of 1942. He trained as an aircraft mechanic. By November of 1942 he was serving as assistant crew chief at MacDill Army Air Field where he worked on bomber aircraft.[98] At some point he was deployed to France where he received the Bronze Star in 1944. By 1945 he was Technical Sergeant Crew Chief with the Silver Streaks Marauder group maintaining bombers that attack Nazi targets.[99] Sterling received a Duty Discharge for medical reasons in October of 1945. In November of 1945 he married his longtime sweetheart, Barbara Daniels. "The marriage of Miss Barbara Daniel, daughter of Mr. and Mrs. L. K. Daniels of Hammond and Sterling A. Kent, son of Mr. and Mrs. Albert Kent of 42 Maple St., the village took place in the rectory of the Catholic church in Rossie on Thursday morning, November 8. Rev. Father Sticklemyer officiated. The bride wore a dark blue velvet dress with fuchsia accessories and a corsage of red roses and 'mums. The brides-maid was gowned in cerise dress with chocolate trimmings. The couple was attended by Miss Beverly Daniels, sister of the bride, and Robert Smith of Potsdam. Mrs. Kent is a graduate of Hammond High School and also of the Wallace Secretarial school in Ogdensburg. She has been employed in the bookkeeping department of the local Montgomery Ward store. Mr. Kent, who was recently discharged from the service where he spent two years overseas with the Ninth Air Force is a graduate of Potsdam High School and was employed by the Ward company before entering the service. They will make their home with Mr. Kent's parents on Maple St., after they return from a trip to Montreal."[100]

"Announcement is made of the marriage of Blanche L. Lauzon, Bennington, Vt., to Orin N. Kent, son of Mr. and Mrs. Albert B. Kent, Maple street, Potsdam, which took place on Tuesday evening, Jan. 20 (1942.) Justice of the Peace John B. Donovan performed the ceremony. Miss Barbara Daniels and Sterling Kent, brother of the groom, attended the couple. Mr. and Mrs. Kent are residing at the Fitzgerald home, 3 Broad St. Mrs. Kent is a nurse on the staff of the Potsdam hospital. Mr. Kent is a graduate of Potsdam high school and the State Normal school class of 1937. He is now associated with the Cook & Kent I.G.A. grocery store in Main street."[101] Orin entered army service for World War II on September 9, 1942. He did his basic training at Camp Upton and was then transferred to Miami Beach, Florida where he worked in finance.[102] Orin's first son was born October 31, 1943. Orin remained in service until after the war ended. "Cpl. Orin Kent, Maple Street, has arrived home following his discharge from the army at Fort Dix, N. J., on Feb. 8 with his wife and

Sterling A. Kent and Barbara Daniels

son, Orin Jr., two years old. Mr. Kent served 13 months overseas, first with the engineers and later with a fighter control squadron. He was in England, France, and Germany during his tour of overseas duty. Entering service in August, 1942, he was awarded the European theatre campaign ribbon with two battle stars, the American theatre campaign ribbon, world war 2 victory medal and the good conduct medal. Mr. Kent arrived in this country at New York on Feb. 3 (1946.) A partner in the Cook and Kent store in Main street, he plans to resume work this week."[103]

Both Orin and Sterling survived the war without being wounded physically. However, according to their mother, they both suffered from shell shock which today is called PTSD.[104]

On June 9, 1947 Orin and Sterling's sister, Alberta Jane, became the second member of her family to graduate from the State Teachers College at Potsdam, Orin having graduated in 1937. She married Gordon David Miller of Massena, New York on August 30, 1948. Gordon had served in the Pacific during World War II. "Miss Alberta Jane Kent, daughter of Mr. and Mrs. Albert B. Kent, Potsdam, and Gordon D. Miller, son of Mr. and Mrs. Clifford Miller, Massena, were married at 9 a.m. onday [sic] in St. Mary's Catholic church by Rev. Joseph L. Tierney, pastor. Miss Vera Miller, Massena, sister of the groom, was maid of honor and Sterling Kent, brother of the bride, was best man. Linda Miller, sister of the groom, was flower girl and Orin Kent, 2nd nephew of the bride, was ring bearer. Orin N. Kent and Orin Miller, brothers of the bride and groom, respectively, were ushers. Miss Barbara Calipari was at the organ and Miss Helen Crump sang three solos. The bride was given in marriage by her father. A wedding breakfast was held at the home of Mr. and Mrs. Sterling Kent after which the couple left on a trip through New England and up the coast of Maine. The bride is a gradu-ate of the Potsdam High school and Potsdam State Teachers College in 1947. She has been a member of the faculty of Washington school in Massena. Miller

Jane Kent and Gordon D. Miller

attended Massena High school and Clarkson College, later serving with the Navy in the Pacific. He is now employed in Schenectady where the couple will reside."[105]

Uncle Johnny, Albert John Kent, died in an accident in 1948. "A ver-dict of accidental death was given by Mrs. Florence Dunlop, coroner, following an inquest in the accident which cost the life of Albert Kent, 81, this village, in Maple St. Monday evening. The inquest was held yesterday afternoon at the local police station. Mr. Kent died at 11:30 p.m. Monday in the Potsdam Hospital, about five hours after the accident, of internal hemorrhages. He also sustained compound fractures of both legs. Kent was struck by a car driven by Lyndon Drake, Bombay, who was proceed-ing west toward Canton. He stopped the car immediately and found the aged man in the road. The accident occurred during a heavy rain in front of the Nickerson gas station in Maple street [sic]. The victim was given first aid at the scene by Dr. M. L. Stevenson and taken to the hospital in the Garner ambulance. He was found to have compound fractures of both legs, facial cuts and bruises. Dr. Watkins attended him at the hospital. He was born in Potsdam in August, 1867, a son of Albert B. and Jane Kent. In his early life he was employed as a tailor in the old Potsdam woolen mills. Later he went to Boston, Mass., and was employed by the state for many years, retiring in 1940. A year later he returned to Potsdam and had since resided with a nephew, Albert Kent, Maple St. Survivors include a sister, Mrs. Herbert Halford, and two nephews, Albert and Charles Kent of Potsdam."[106]

Albert B. Kent died November 28, 1950 from an asthmatic and heart condition at Potsdam Hospital.[107] "Funeral services for Albert Kent, 60, resident of this village for many years, who died in the Potsdam hospital on Tuesday morning will be held from St. Mary's church Thursday morning at 9 a.m. with Rev. Joseph L. Tierney, pastor officiating and burial will be made in St. Mary's cemetery. Mr. Kent was born in Augusta, Maine on September 3, 1890, a son of Charles and Minnie Kent. He moved to Potsdam as a young man and has been employed for the past 11 years at the Aluminum plant as a machinist. He married the former Kate Gardner 38 years ago. He was a member of the Potsdam council of the K. of C. Surviving besides his wife is one daughter, Mrs. Gordon (Jane) Miller of Potsdam, two sons Orin and Sterling, both of Potsdam and one brother Charles of Potsdam. Five grandchildren also survive. Pall bearers will be Maurice Gibson, Gerald Bockus, Al Driscoil, George Smith, Pat Walsh and Orin Miller. Funeral arrangements are in charge of the George A Gardner Funeral Home."[108]

Albert Byron Kent

Orin Nelson Kent
1913-1986

. . . .

Albert Byron Kent
1890-1950
Katherine Newcomb Gardner
1895-1990

Sterling Albert Kent
1920-1986

. . . .

Alberta Jane Kent
1925-2005

Katherine Gardner Kent Family History

Katherine Newcomb Gardner Kent's family background began with her grandmother Catherine Command [Cammins, Commans] who immigrated from Newcastle West, Limerick, Ireland in 1845 at the age of about seven.[109] 1845 coincides with the beginning of the Irish Potato Famine, or, as some call it, the Irish Genocide.[110] The wooden, sail powered ships that brought the Irish to America and Canada at the beginning of the famine were probably a bit better than the overcrowded, disease ridden ships that followed as the famine intensified. Those later ships were nicknamed "the coffin ships."[111]

There are at least three versions of who accompanied Catherine on her journey. One says that she traveled with her sister.[112] Another says that she came with an aunt.[113] The third says that she arrived with an uncle and aunt.[114] There are no Ellis Island records as that emigrant processing place did not open until 1892. One source says she disembarked at Troy, NY.[115] Troy was a popular destination for immigrants from several European countries.[116]

By age twelve Catherine was in Gouverneur, NY where she was employed by Rev. Sawyer, pastor of the First Baptist church. Later she lived with the attorney C. A. Parker family.[117] On January 2, 1854 Catherine married William Newcomb, a carpenter.[118] She was only sixteen, but it was common for the Irish to marry early at that time.[119] On March 17, 1854 William, who was about 20 at the time, died in the Oswegatchie River. "Dear Sir-I hasten to inform you of a sad calamity which occurred at this place yesterday, by which three men, O.C. Hill, William Newcomb, and William Broderick, lost their lives. The circumstances are briefly as follows: They were enjoying a pleasure ride in a yawl boat, just below the mill dam in this Village. It appears they tried to see how near they could approach the dam with safety, when the bow of the boat was caught by the current, and in spite of their efforts, they were drawn into the whirlpool caused by the falling waters. They remained in the boat till it was nearly filled, then jumped out. Two of them immediately sunk and did not rise again: the third caught hold of a piece of ice and floated for several minutes. Boards were thrown to him but being some distance from shore, did not reach him. He maintained his hold on the piece of ice, till it came in contact with another, when he was compelled to let go, and instantly sank. The above facts I obtained from an eye witness. The water being very high and running swiftly, and not having a boat of sufficient size and strength, it was impossible to afford them much assistance. Their bodies have not been recovered, although the ice was cleared for a considerable distance in the vicinity; it will be difficult to rake the river the bottom being uneven. Mr. Hill was in all respects a worthy man, and his loss will be deeply felt in the community. He leaves a wife and three children to mourn his untimely end. Mr. Newcomb also leaves a wife."[120] Catherine was pregnant at the time of William's death and her only daughter, Anna, was born December 8, 1854.[121]

On October 4, 1857 Catherine married John Dusharm in the Methodist church in Gouverneur.[122] He was one of twelve children born to Francois Dusharm and Marie Riel of Canada who moved from Contrecoeur, Quebec south to the Plattsburg, NY area around 1838. John was actually born in Chazy, NY in 1836. Catherine and John's first son, John, was born in 1858. Their first set of twin boys were born August 1, 1860. On August 28, 1862 John enlisted in the Union Army leaving Catherine at home with four children and another on the way.

John served in the 1st New York Light Artillery, Battery D and was in the number one position of his crew which fired 12 pound Napoleon cannons. Battery D took part in many Civil War battles including Fredericksburg, Chancellorsville, Gettysburg, the Wilderness, Spotsylvania Court House, Cold Harbor and Five Forks. They were present at Appomattox Court House at the surrender of Lee. Battery D mustered out May 30, 1865.[123] John returned to his hometown of Gouverneur without suffering any battle wounds. Ironically, on July 4, 1874 he served on a gun crew firing shots from a canon to celebrate the holiday. The canon misfired and John lost his right arm.[124]

After the war, John returned to Gouverneur where he worked as a laborer. Later on the family farmed in Pitcairn, NY, finally returning to Gouverneur by 1915. By 1873 the family included eight sons as the youngest had died in a drowning accident in the same river that Catherine's first husband had died in. John passed away June 24, 1924. "John Dusharm, a long time [sic] resident of this village and a Civil War vet, died suddenly at his home in Read street [sic] last night. He was well known and had passed his 80th year. Several years ago well in firing off a cannon at the rear of the E. D. Barry establishment in Clinton street, which is now occupied by the Spooner-Campbell company, the cannon exploded and Mr. Dusharm lost one of his arms. He was a member of Barnes Post G. A. R. Old age in these later years had prevented him from being active and to which he finally succumbed. Mr. Dusharm is survived by his widow, several children and 34 grandchildren. The funeral will be held Friday morning and burial made in Riverside."[125]

"Mrs. Catherine Command Dusharm died at the age of 92 years at the home of her son, James Dusharm, on Smith street [sic] Friday morning after an illness of three months. Despite her advanced age, she had been in fairly good health until about Christmas time when she was taken ill. She was the widow of the late John Dusharm whose death occurred about three years ago. Mrs. Dusharm was born in County Cork Ireland, the daughter of John and Nora Reardon Command, and came to this country at the age of nine years with and aunt and came to Gouverneur when she was about twelve years of age, since which time she has been a resident here. Upon moving to Gouverneur she was employed at the residence of Rev. Conant Sawyer, then pastor of the First Baptist church. She later lived with C. A. Parker, father of the present C. A. Parker, local attorney. She was married from the Parker home her first husband being William Newcomb, one daughter being born, Mrs. Joseph Gardner, whose death occurred a year ago. Her second husband was the late John Dusharm. Her first husband was drowned 74 years ago on St. Patrick's Day. The survivors include six sons, Charles Dusharm, Harrisville, William Dusharm, Hermon, Hiram, James, Albert, and Walter Dusharm all residents of this village. She had 40 grandchildren, 52 great grandchildren and three great great

Catherine Command

Catherine's Second Husband John Dusharm

grandchildren. Funeral services were held Monday morning at the St. James Catholic church at ten o'clock, the pastor Rev. M. F. Gallivan officiating and burial was made in Riverside cemetery."[126]

William Newcomb
1834-1854
Catherine Command
1838-1927

Anna Newcomb
1854-1925

John Dusharm
1858-1870

Charles Dusharm
1861-1951

Chester Dusharm
1861-1916

William Dusharm
1863-1944

John Dusharm
1836-1924
Catherine Command Newcomb
1838-1927

Hiram Dusharm
1866-1929

James Dusharm
1867-1958

Albert Dusharm
1871-?

Wallace Dusharm
1873-1923

Walter Dusharm
1873-1944

Anna Newcomb lived with her mother and step-father and eight step-brothers until her marriage to Joseph Nelson Gardner in 1873 at age eighteen. Ironically, Joseph was also raised by a step-father. Joseph was born in Massena Springs Hamlet in 1853.[127] His father's first name is not known. His mother's maiden name was Mary Cannell. Joseph's father was a wood cutter in the Black Lake area of New York. When Joseph was young, his father went missing in that wilderness. His mother remarried to Nicholas Pare [Pair] and bore five more sons. At a young age, Joseph began working at the grist mill in Gouverneur.

Joseph's Maternal Grandmother Mary Cannell

Joseph and Anna were married in the Presbyterian church in Gouverneur on November 13, 1873.[128] They had nine children during their fifty-two year marriage, however only four lived until old age.

Charles died at age six. "The missing boy, Charles Gardner, was found this morning in one of the buckets of the Graves grist mill. The body was badly mangled, having been in the wheel since March 15th, and the mill running all the time. It was a sad sight. He followed his father and Mr. Lawrence, the miller, down

Joseph's Mother
Mary Cannell Gardner Pare [Pair]

below, and fell through an opening of about 20 inches into the bulkhead."[129] By 1900 Joseph no longer worked at the grist mill, but was working as a stone mason.[130]

Lula Belle, Nora, and Mammie Rose all died of consumption (tuberculosis.) "Last Saturday evening at her home on the Brooklyn side, occurred the death of Mrs. Nora Gardner Beauchaine, aged 21 years, after an illness of eight months with consumption."[131]

Florence passed in Watertown, NY as a result of the Spanish Flu epidemic of 1918. "Mrs. Florence Ethel Clobridge, wife of Edward J. Clobridge, died at the family home, 405 Stone street [sic] between 4 and 5 Saturday night, following a week's illness of influenza and pneumonia, aged 29 years. She was taken ill Saturday, Oct. 19 and her condition during the past three days had been [?]. She was born in Gouverneur, daughter of Joseph and Anna Gardner and spent her early life in that village, coming to this city about eleven years ago. She married Edward J. Clobridge eleven years ago. Besides her husband, she leaves four sons, Robert, aged ten years, Paul, aged seven, Edward, aged four, and Ralph, aged two. Her parents, Mr. and Mrs. Joseph Gardner of Gouverneur, also survive with three brothers, Irvin, William and Clarence, all of Gouverneur and one sister, Mrs. Albert Kent of this city. She was a member of the Stone Street Presbyterian church. The funeral will be held Tuesday afternoon from the residence 405 Stone street [sic], privately. Interment will be in Brookside cemetery.[132]

Anna Newcomb Gardner died December 7, 1925. "Mrs. Joseph N. Gardner, a life long resident of Gouverneur, died Monday at the home of her daughter, Mrs. Albert Kent, in Syracuse where she had been since July on account of ill health. Her maiden name was Anna Newcomb, and she was born in Gouverneur Dec. 8, 1853 and at the time of her death lacked but a day of being 72 years old. Her father was drowned in the Oswegatchie river and her mother a few years afterward married John Dusharm. Mrs. Gardner is survived by her husband, Joseph Gardner, three sons, Irvan and William of Gouverneur, Clarence of Syracuse, and one daughter, Mrs. Albert Kent, of Syracuse, also by her aged mother, Mrs. Dusharm of Read street [sic], and by several half brothers. The remains arrived in Gouverneur last evening, and were taken to the family home at No. 106 Parker street [sic], from where the funeral will be held Thursday afternoon at 2:30, internment following in Riverside cemetery."[133]

By 1930 Joseph was boarding with Minnie Kent at 38 Maple Street. Albert and Kate Kent, their three children and two other borders were also living there.[134] Joseph was living with Albert, Kate and their children in the home they had acquired from Elizabeth "Nellie" Kent at 42 Maple street when he died on December 13, 1938. "Joseph N. Gardner died Tuesday morning at the home of his daughter, Mrs. Albert Kent, Maple St. with whom he had made his home for the past three years. Mr. Gardner was born at Massena Springs, Nov. 19, 1853 but moved to Gouverneur when young and worked for 30 years in the old grist mill on West Main St., and later worked as a stone mason. On Nov. 13, 1873 he married Miss Anna M. Newcomb of Gouverneur who died Dec. 8, 1925. He is survived by his daughter, Mrs. Albert Kent of Potsdam; three sons, Irvin N. Gardner and William H. Gardner of Gouverneur and Clarence

Gardner of Macomb. Funeral services were held at the Sprague Funeral Home in Gouverneur, Thursday afternoon, Rev. V.O. Boyle officiating with burial in Riverside cemetery."[135]

Joseph N. Gardner and Anna Newcomb 1873

Irvon N. Gardner
1874-1946

. . . .

Nora Gardner
1876-1897

. . . .

Charles Gardner
1878-1884

. . . .

Lula Belle Gardner
1880-1895

. . . .

Joseph Nelson Gardner
1853-1938
Anna Newcomb
1854-1925

William Gardner
1882-1970

. . . .

Clarence L. Gardner
1887-1970

. . . .

Florence E. Gardner
1889-1918

. . . .

Katherine N. Gardner
1895-1990

. . . .

Mammie Rose Gardner
1897-1900

Left to right-William, Clarence, and Irvon Gardner

Nora Gardner

Clarence Leo Gardner and Eva Ellen Savage were married April 4, 1908. Clarence was quite the prankster as a young man according to his sister, Katherine. He also played the blues harmonica. Clarence and Eva had no children of their own. Clarence had a terrible farm accident in the spring of 1955 when he was dragged by a team of horses. He spent the rest of his life as a hunchback.

That's a1936 prize winning turkey.

Florence Gardner loved those big hats.

Katherine Newcomb Gardner about 1912

Katherine Gardner Kent

Endnotes

1   Fiske, J. F. (2008 and 2009). The English Background of Richard Kent Sr. and
    Stephen Kent of Newbury, Massachusetts, Mary, Wife of Nicholas Easton of
    Newport, Rhode Island, *The New England Historical and Genealogical Register*
    (162) pp.245-55 and *The New England Historical and Genealogical Register*
    (163) pp.159-71. [All information to this point is from these articles.]

2   U.S., New England Marriages Prior to 1700

3   VIRKUS, F. A., editor. (1964). *Immigrant Ancestors: A List of 2,500 Immigrants
    to America before 1750*. Baltimore: Genealogical Publishing Co., p.75

4   Anderson, R. C. (2005). *The Great Migration Immigrants to New England
    1634-1635, Vol. 4* .Boston, MA: New England Historic Genealogical Society
    p. 142

5   George Sheldon, (1896). *A History of Deerfield, Massachusetts: the times when
    the people by whom it was settled, unsettled and resettled*. Greenfield, MA: Press
    of E.A. Hall & Co., p. 892

6   Seversmith, H.F. (1953). *Colonial Families of Long Island, New York, and
    Connecticut Being the Ancestry and Kindred of Herbert Furman Seversmith Vol. 4.*
    Washington, D.C. p. 1678

7   Pringle, J. R. (1892). *History of the Town and City of Gloucester, Cape Ann,
    Massachusetts*. Gloucester, MA: Published by the Author, p. 38

8   Ancestry.com. (2012). *U.S., Find A Grave Index, 1600s-Current* [database on-
    line]. Provo, UT, USA: Ancestry.com Operations, Inc.,

9   Edmund West, comp. (2001). *Family Data Collection – Deaths* [database on-
    line]. Provo, UT, USA: Ancestry.com Operations Inc.

10 Heritage Consulting. (2003). *Millennium File* [database on-line]. Provo, UT,
    USA: Ancestry.com Operations Inc.

11 Ancestry.com. (2012). *U.S., Find A Grave Index, 1600s-Current* [database on-
    line]. Provo, UT, USA: Ancestry.com Operations, Inc.

12 Edmund West, comp. (2001). *Family Data Collection – Marriages* [database on-line]. Provo, UT, USA: Ancestry.com Operations Inc.

13 Roy, l. E., M.D. (1965). *Quaboag Plantation alias Brookefeild.* West Brookfield, Mass. : Self Published, p. 161

14 Chase, E. (May 2014) Samuel Sr. and Samuel Kent Jr., Original Suffield Proprietors. *Stony Brook Currents, Volume IX* (No. 2)Retrieved from http://www.suffieldhistoricalsociety.org

15 Roy, L. E., M.D., (1965).*Quaboag Plantation alias Brookefeild* West Brookfield, Mass. : Self Published p. 264

16 Roy, L. E., M.D., (1965).*Quaboag Plantation alias Brookefeild* West Brookfield, Mass. : Self Published p. 265

17 Brooks, R. B. (2017, May 31). History of King Philip's War. History of Massachusetts Blog. Retrieved from https://historyofmassachusetts.org/what-was-king-philips-war/

18 Family History of Samuel Kent (n.d.) Retrieved from http://www.suffieldhistoricalsociety.org

19 Roy, L.E., M.D., (1965). *Quaboag Plantation alias Brookefeild.* West Brookfield, Mass. : Self Published, p. 267

20 Cutter, W.R. (1910). *Genealogical and Family History of Northern New York Vol. II.* New York, Lewis Historical Publishing Company, p. 532

21 James Kent From the New York Tribune. (1847, December 15). Albany Evening Journal. Albany, NY. Vol. 18. Issue 5385. p.2. Retrieved from https://www.genealogybank.com

22 Family History of Lancelot Granger (n.d.) Retrieved from http://www.suffieldhistoricalsociety.org

23 History.com Editors, (updated Feb. 6, 2002). French and Indian War. Retrieved from https//www.history.com

24 CT Historical Society. (1903). *Roles of Connecticut Men in the French and Indian War 1755-1762Vol. I and II* Hartford: Connecticut Historical Society. pp. 103, 6, and 102

25 Lanesborough, Massachusetts, Early Lanesborough Settlers (n.d.) Retrieved from http://www.earlyamericanancestors.com/surnames/kent/abel1.html

26   Lanesborough, Massachusetts, Early Lanesborough Settlers (n.d.) Retrieved
      from earlyamericanancestors.com/locations/lanesborough

27   Lanesborough, Massachusetts, Early Lanesborough Settlers (2012, July)
      Retrieved from earlyamericanancestors.com/locations/lanesborough/
      affairhtml

28   Lanesborough, Massachusetts, Early Lanesborough Settlers (2012, July)
      Retrieved from earlyamericanancestors.com/locations/Lanesborough/
      affair2html

29   Massachusetts. (1896-1908). Secretary of the Commonwealth. *Massachusetts
      Soldiers and Sailors of the Revolutionary War. Vol.9.* Boston, MA, USA: Wright
      & Potter Printing, p. 135

30   Bagg, M. M. (1877). *The Pioneers of Utica: Being Sketches of Its Inhabitants and
      Its Institutions, With the Civil History of the Place from the Earliest Settlement to
      the Year 1825-the Era of the Opening of the Erie Canal.* Utica, NY: Curtis and
      Childs, Printers and Publishers p. 30

31   New York, Tax Assessment Rolls of Real and Personal Estates, 1799-1804 for
      Noah Kent Oneida 1800 Rome

32   Durant, S. W. (1878). *History of Oneida County, New York: with illustrations
      and biographical sketches of some of its prominent men and pioneers.* Philadelphia:
      Everts & Fariss p. 450

33   *War of 1812 abstracts of payrolls for New York State militia ("payroll cards"),
      1812–1814.* Series B0810 (23.5 cu. ft.). New York (State). Adjutant General's
      Office. New York State Archives, Albany, New York. P. 983-986

34   *War of 1812 abstracts of payrolls for New York State militia ("payroll cards"),
      1812–1814.*

35   U.S. General Land Office Records, 1776-2015 for Orrin Kent Illinois, Lake

36   State of Illinois. (1999). *Illinois, Public Land Purchase Records, 1813-1909*
      [database on-line]. Provo, UT, USA: Ancestry.com Operations Inc.,

37   U.S. General Land Office Records, 1776-2015 for Orrin Kent Illinois, Lake

38   1850 United States Federal Census

39   Oregon, Biographical and Other Index Card File, 1700s-1900s for Horace
      Ayrault Kent Pioneer Index

40   1850 United States Federal Census

41 Illinois, Marriage Index, 1860-1920

42 1900 United States Federal Census

43 1850 United States Federal Census

44 Darius A. Kant in the Michigan, Deaths and Burials Index, 1867-1995

45 *Marriage Records. Michigan Marriages.* Various Michigan County marriage collections.

46 Ancestry.com. (2009). *1860 United States Federal Census* [database on-line]. Provo, UT, USA: Ancestry.com Operations, Inc.

47 Michigan, Death Records, 1897-1920 and Ancestry.com. (2011). *Michigan, Deaths and Burials Index, 1867-1995* [database on-line]. Provo, UT, USA: Ancestry.com Operations, Inc.

48 *Lake County, Illinois probate packets, 1840-1900*; Author: *Illinois. County Court (Lake County)*; Probate

49 1850 United States Federal Census

50 Familysearch.org

51 1850 United States Federal Census for Benjamin Gardner New York Oneida Floyd

52 2013,13 May email to Patricia Mihok from Dawna Holst

53 1850 United States Federal Census for Benjamin Gardner New York Oneida Floyd

54 Ancestry.com. (2000). *Wisconsin, Marriage Index, 1820-1907* [database on-line]. Provo, UT, USA: Ancestry.com Operations, Inc.

55 1850 United States Federal Census for O S Kent Wisconsin Green Sylvester

56 Washington State and Territorial Censuses, 1857-1892 for C A Kent 1887 San Juan Lopez Island

57 Ancestry.com. (2014). *Washington, Select Death Certificates, 1907-1960* [database on-line]. Provo, UT, USA: Ancestry.com Operations, Inc.

58 1850 United States Federal Census for Albert Kent New York Oneida Floyd

59 Kent Family Lineage Tree, on five eight inch by ten inch newsprint sheets taped together with browning clear tape, one sheet is missing. Given to the author by her mother.

60   1860 United States Federal Census for Albert Kent New York, Broome, Binghamton Ward 5

61   Historical Data Systems, comp. (2009). *U.S., Civil War Soldier Records and Profiles, 1861-1865* [database on-line]. Provo, UT, USA: Ancestry.com Operations Inc.

62   Wisconsin Historical Society, 13th Wisconsin Infantry History (n.d.) Retrieved from www.wisconsinhistory.org/Records/Article/CS2218

63   National Archives & Records Admin. CIVIL WAR Military Service Veterans Record & Pension Application

64   2013, 13 May email to Patricia Mihok from Dawna Holst

65   National Archives & Records Admin. CIVIL WAR Military Service Veterans Record & Pension Application

66   1870 United States Federal Census for Charles Kent New York, Saint Lawrence, Potsdam

67   Albert Kent and Libbie Kent's Certificates of Baptism are in the procession of the author.

68   1900 United States Federal Census for Peter Counter New York Saint Lawrence Potsdam

69   1900 United States Federal Census

70   Kent Family Lineage Tree, on five eight inch by ten inch newsprint sheets taped together with browning clear tape, one sheet is missing. Given to the author by her mother.

71   1910 United States Federal Census

72   New York, State Census, 1915 for Albert B Kent St Lawrence Potsdam

73   New York, Death Index, 1852-1956 for June Counter New York State Department of Health 1920

74   (2011). Seven Members of the 13th Wisconsin Volunteer Infantry Company K[Photograph]. Retrieved from www.wisconsinhistory.org

75   1880 United States Federal Census for Charles O. Kent New York St Lawrence Gouverneur 253

76   Note given to the author by her mother.

77   New York State, Marriage Index, 1881-1967

78 Katherine Kent, interviewed by Bruce and Debbie Kent, 42 Maple Street, Potsdam, NY, September 1989, videotape converted to CD in procession of the author.

79 Kent Family Lineage Tree, on five eight inch by ten inch newsprint sheets taped together with browning clear tape, one sheet is missing. Given to the author by her mother.

80 New York, Passenger Lists, 1820-1957

81 Albert Kent's Baptismal Certificated is in the possession of the Author.

82 1900 United States Federal Census for Albert B Kent New York Saint Lawrence Potsdam

83 New York State, Birth Index, 1881-1942, New York, Death Index, 1880-1956

84 1910 United States Federal Census

85 Charles O. Kent. (1927, February 4). *The Potsdam Herald – recorder*. p.4. Retrieved from https://nyshistoricnewspapers.org/

86 1910 United States Federal Census for Albert B Kent New York Saint Lawrence Potsdam

87 New York, County Marriage Records, 1847-1849, 1907-1936 for Albert Byron Kent St Lawrence 1908 – 1915

88 Kent-Gardner. (1913, February 5). *Gouverneur Free Press*, p. 2. Retrieved from https://nyshistoricnewspapers.org/

89 U.S. WWII Draft Cards Young Men, 1940-1947 for Orin Nelson Kent New York (State) Jendrian-Latak Kent, Jerome-Kerekes, Andrew

90 U.S., World War I Draft Registration Cards, 1917-1918 for Albert Byron Kent New York Jefferson County 1 Draft Card K

91 New York, State Census, 1925 for Albert B Kent Onondaga Syracuse Ward 18 A.D. 02 E.D. 05

92 Conversations with Katherine N. Kent and the author.

93 1930 United States Federal Census for Albert B Kent New York Saint Lawrence Potsdam District 0081

94 Agreement as to Deposition of properties of Halford and Halford and care of Elizabeth Kent Halford Elizabeth Kent Halford, first party Herbert Halford, second party Albert B. Kent and Katherine Gardner Kent, third parties, in possession of the author.

95   (1938, December 14). *Courier and Freeman*. p.15. Retrieved from https://nyshistoricnewspapers.org/

96   U.S., World War II Draft Registration Cards, 1942 for Albert Byron Kent New York

97   The photograph of Orin and Sterling Kent in uniform taken at Miami Beach, Florida in 1942 is in the procession of the author.

98   Kent Brothers Meet in Miami, Florida. (1942, November 11). *Courier and freeman*. p.3. Retrieved from https://nyshistoricnewspapers.org/

99   (1945, April 4). *Courier and Freeman*. p.9. Retrieved from https://nyshistoricnewspapers.org/

100   Barbara Daniels, Bride of War Vet. (1945, November 14). *Courier and freeman*. p. 5. Retrieved from https://nyshistoricnewspapers.org/

101   Orin Kent and Blanche Lauzon Wed Jan. 20 (1942,January 28). *Courier and Freeman*. p.3. Retrieved from https://nyshistoricnewspapers.org/

102   Kent Brothers Meet in Miami, Florida. (1942, November 11). *Courier and freeman*. p.3. Retrieved from https://nyshistoricnewspapers.org/

103   Orin Kent Released From Army Service. (1946, February 20). *Courier and freeman*. p. 1. Retrieved from https://nyshistoricnewspapers.org/

104   Conversations with Katherine N. Kent and the author.

105   Kent-Miller Nuptials Held. (1948, September 1). *The Potsdam Herald-recorder*, p.5. Retrieved from https://nyshistoricnewspapers.org/

106   Man, 81, Hit by Car, Dies. (1948, November 24). *Potsdam herald-recorder*. p.1. Retrieved from https://nyshistoricnewspapers.org/

107   (1950, November 30). *The Massena Observer*. p.4. Retrieved from https://nyshistoricnewspapers.org/

108   (1950, November 29). *The Potsdam Herald-recorder*. p.12. Retrieved from https://nyshistoricnewspapers.org/

109   1920 United States Federal Census for Catherine Ducharm New York Saint Lawrence Gouverneur District 0127

110   Coogan, T. M. (2013). *The Famine Plot*. New York, New York: St. Martin's Griffin

111   Coogan, T. M. (2013). *The Famine Plot*. New York, New York: St. Martin's Griffin

112 Katherine Kent, interviewed by Bruce and Debbie Kent, 42 Maple Street, Potsdam, NY, September 1989, videotape converted to CD in procession of the author.

113 Mrs. Catherine Dusharm. (1927, March 23). *The Northern Tribune*, p. 4. Retrieved from https://nyshistoricnewspapers.org/

114 Dusharm-Villeneuve, C. E. (2008, June). My Great-Grandfather John Dusharm and the Civil War. *Le Trait d' Union, Vol. 15*, pp.13-14

115 Katherine Kent, interviewed by Bruce and Debbie Kent, 42 Maple Street, Potsdam, NY, September 1989, videotape converted to CD in procession of the author.

116 Young, Esq., P. (2018). Women of Troy (N.Y.): The Teenaged Irish Immigrants Who Started the First Permanent Women's Union in the Middle of the Civil War. *Long Island Wins*, retrieved from https://longislandwins.com

117 Mrs. Catherine Dusharm. (1927, March 23). *The Northern Tribune*, p. 4. Retrieved from https://nyshistoricnewspapers.org/

118 Katherine Kent, interviewed by Bruce and Debbie Kent, 42 Maple Street, Potsdam, NY, September 1989, videotape converted to CD in procession of the author.

119 Coogan, T. M. (2013). *The Famine Plot*. New York, New York: St. Martin's Griffin

120 S. Foote, Esq. (1854, March 21). Gouverneur, Saturday, March 18. *The Ogdensburgh Sentinel*. p.2. Retrieved from https://nyshistoricnewspapers.org/

121 1900 United States Federal Census for Anna Gardner New York Saint Lawrence Gouverneur

122 Dusharm-Villeneuve, C. E. (2008, June). My Great-Grandfather John Dusharm and the Civil War. *Le Trait d' Union, Vol. 15*, pp.13-14

123 New York, Civil War Muster Roll Abstracts, 1861-19001st Artillery (Light) D-FLIED654

124 Dusharm-Villeneuve, C. E. (2008, June). My Great-Grandfather John Dusharm and the Civil War. *Le Trait d' Union, Vol. 15*, pp.13-14

125 John Dusharm Civil War Vet Died Last Night, Succumbed to Ravages of Old Age-Had Resided here Many Years-Lost Arm While Firing Cannon One Fourth of July Morning-Was Well Known. (1924, June 25). *Gouverneur Free Press*, p.1. Retrieved from https://nyshistoricnewspapers.org/

126 Mrs. Catherine Dusharm. (1927, March 23). *The Northern Tribune*. p. 4. Retrieved from https://nyshistoricnewspapers.org/

127 Joseph N. Gardner. (1938,December 16). *The Potsdam Herald-recorder*. p. 6. Retrieved from https://nyshistoricnewspapers.org/

128 Joseph N. Gardner and Anna Newcomb's Marriage Certificate is in procession of the author.

129 Gouverneur. (1884, April 5). *The Ogdensburg Journal*. p. 3. Retrieved from https://nyshistoricnewspapers.org/

130 1900 United States Federal Census for Joseph Gardner New York Saint Lawrence Gouverneur District 0093

131 (1897, April 14). *The Northern Tribune*. p. 5. Retrieved from https://nyshistoricnewspapers.org/

132 Mrs. Florence Clobridge. (1918, October 28). *Watertown Daily Times*. p.10. Retrieved from https://nyshistoricnewspapers.org/

133 Mrs. Joseph Gardner Died In Syracuse. (1925, December 9). *Gouverneur Free Press*. p. 1. Retrieved from https://nyshistoricnewspapers.org/

134 1930 United States Federal Census for Joseph N Gardner New York Saint Lawrence Potsdam District 0081

135 Joseph N. Gardner. (1938, December 16). *The Potsdam Herald-recorder*. p. 6. Retrieved from https://nyshistoricnewspapers.org/

www.ingramcontent.com/pod-product-compliance
Lightning Source LLC
Chambersburg PA
CBHW070116070426
42448CB00040B/3042